Are You a Unicorn or Are You a Rhino
Do You Feel Inspired or Just Motivated?

A Single Page-a-Day Primer for Leaders

by
Randy Zeyen

Copyright © 2020 by Randy Zeyen
All rights reserved. This book or any portion thereof may
not be reproduced or used in any manner whatsoever
without the written permission of the author.

Introduction

"You can do the work of two people, but you can't be two people. Instead, you have to inspire the next guy down the line and get him to inspire his people."
Lee Iacocca

I love these words by the great auto guru, Lee Iacocca. Among all American business icons, he is one of my personal favorites. He possessed what you might envision in a revolutionary American entrepreneur. His fantastic career merged engineer, designer, salesman, marketing genius, and a guy with plenty of guts. I am not alone in my belief that he was the exemplary balance between humility and courage. This quote at the top of the page reveals quite a bit about how this guy viewed his work. There hasn't been a decision-maker anything quite like him in multiple decades. He was one who could do everything himself, start-to-finish, and yet, he clearly understood the value of bringing others along, each with their own unique talents.

Some of the world's finest leaders have matured into historical heroes by teaching others to take his or her place.

If you've read any of my earlier volumes, you'll already know that I believe in how branding and leadership go hand in hand. I love to help energize great brands, in particular because they can also grow to become corporate leaders. I've been aware that by studying the way in which people learn, the way in which they make some of life's simplest decisions, might help enable me to become better at product design, promotion, marketing, branding, and of course leading.

In addition to understanding this, it might also help me to enrich the lives of others. This isn't just a campaign slogan. At least for me, connecting people to products they love, is not a tactic, it is a joy I love.

I look for ways to inspire others. I do this for them, for the people they might also come into contact, and for myself too. I see inspiration as one small candle, that when combined with others, turn into a larger flame. Although my principal job has been be to design, sell, market, and brand products, my passion has always been to make long-lasting connections to people and their products. These are products that people learn to love because they use them in their close relationships with others.

Besides this single, unequalled quote that I shared by Mr. Iacocca, all of the others used in this volume have been collected from wither a speech, or from one of my books that has been published.

Unlike all the others, I wanted this one volume to be easy to read, to put down, and even easier to pick up again. It was designed to read just a single page a day, or less, if you haven't the time. Just one quote and a small paragraph explanation that I am hopeful will inspire you to better dreams, better careers, and better relationships.

Thank you for reading, "Unicorn or Rhino". If this is your first book of mine, I'm very happy it is this one. I hope you enjoy it, and that it inspires you to better things.

Randy Z

Randy Z

About the Author

Randy Z has found it a great privilege to be an innovative force in contributing and guiding a number of dynamic, electrified and connected world brands. He is known as an award-winning designer, and an enthusiastic multidisciplinary brand veteran.

He has has the pleasure of mentoring others and written on this subject for well over three decades. RandyZ is passionate about writing on a variety of topics, including diversity, the purpose of a creative life, and the stratagem of power branding and a connected leadership.

Are You a Unicorn or Are You a Rhino
Do You Feel Inspired or Just Motivated?

A Single Page-a-Day Primer for Leaders

by
Randy Zeyen

Unlike all of my other books, this volume, I call "Unicorn or Rhino", was written for you to read a single page per day or week. I wanted this one to be easy for you to read. I am hopeful it will inspire you to better dreams, better careers, even more importantly, better relationships.

Are You a Unicorn or Are You a Rhino
Do You Feel Inspired or Just Motivated?

One Hundred Daily Quotes
One hundred thoughts

to inspire your day
to make life easier
to learn to listen
to learn to trust
to build your faith
to admit your flaws
to stand your ground

by
Randy Zeyen

1

"In life, we learn to become either a unicorn or a rhinoceros. We inspire or we motivate. We lead or we are reduced to compel."

Leading will always begin and end with inspiration. Only the inspired can create an enthusiastic esprit de corps. Your customers and co-workers must believe that you are passionate, and you have their very best interest at heart. A revolutionary leader will be required to learn to inspire. Once you discover how to merge your passion with compassion, you'll find it so much easier to rouse those around you. Once you do, they will give you their trust, captivated by your compassionate zeal, joyously following you as a leader.

Unicorn or Rhino - Do You Feel Inspired or Just Motivated?

2

"Humanity loves beginnings even more than it does beautiful endings."

We love movies with happy endings. Our human proclivity, is to begin and to end things in a positive way. But, although we may begin life beautifully, human events can change our lives hastily and horribly. Life can go dreadfully wrong. This may reveal why we're not very good at commitment. We begin events with a high degree of stability. but we never expect the good to last. Beginning is always easier. This may reveal why we love beginnings, even more than we do joyful endings. A good start is something in life many of us can count upon.

Unicorn or Rhino - Do You Feel Inspired or Just Motivated?

3

> "With your back against the stoney wall, you are blessed with the best perspective for your future that you could ever hope to visualize."

All of us have been through hard times. All of us. When you feel that life can't get much worse, we also know that it can, and it certainly might. It can become terrible. Our tendency is usually to follow our tragedy down the muddy hole, and live in there with it. We recline in our anxiety even as we flail around. It is all perspective isn't it? If you happen to land in a puddle, step out and clean up your shoes. If you're pressed against a wall and can't see your future, your vision isn't impaired, you're looking the wrong way. You're staring at the wall.

Unicorn or Rhino - Do You Feel Inspired or Just Motivated?

4

"Don't let others mislead you, friends are extremely important. It doesn't take great intelligence to influence others or to make money, it takes connections."

We work hard to climb the ladder of success to achieve because we desire a good life. We love having our friends and family around us, and we want them to do well also. Science tells us that this is a very powerful biological stress-reducer. Being around friends lowers our blood pressure and can add years to our lives. The big surprise is that, being calm and composed will add years to the lives of your friends also! When you stay connected with them, both of you will be healthier and happier. So, keep them close to you.

Unicorn or Rhino - Do You Feel Inspired or Just Motivated?

5

"Happiness is a choice."

I can hear how naive this must sound while I write it down, even though I know it to be true. Sometimes the truth can sound phony-baloney, like it came from a Cracker Jacks box, or a bogus time-share seminar. But, this one is a reliable truth. Happiness is a choice. Our choice. We can choose to be happy, content, or sad whenever events happen in our life. Machines cannot. Unlike human beings, robots calculate prescribed options, and then follow the threads faithfully. They do not choose, we can. Never allow yourself to become captive. You choose your path.

Unicorn or Rhino - Do You Feel Inspired or Just Motivated?

6

> "I'd much rather inspire than motivate. Inspiration elevates, while having to constantly motivate quickly becomes a repetitious, and arduous task."

I once had a student who sat in the back of class drawing severed heads on paper with a pencil. He grew to revel in this anti-social celebrity. Even more interesting to me was that his attention to detail was quite remarkable. When I asked to see his drawings after class, I could tell that his expectation of me was to see my worst impersonation of a teacher. But instead, I critiqued his artwork without commenting on the subject matter. A little confused and yet delighted, a transformation began that day; not to his art, but within him.

Unicorn or Rhino - Do You Feel Inspired or Just Motivated?

7

"Innovation is the product of diversity, not just a reaction to it."

I've never been good at juggling. There are very few of us that are good at it. When people speak in terms of innovation and diversity, they tend to see them as separate and exclusive challenges, circling them in the air. They are so wrong! This may be why we struggle (or we try to juggle them), and we work ourselves so very hard but end up achieving nothing. Take a look at every victorious revolutionary venture in history. Diversity was one of their core principles, while the products of it have been innovation, creativity, and success.

Unicorn or Rhino - Do You Feel Inspired or Just Motivated?

8

"Life is full of important decisions. Resolve if you wish to be the carrot or a stick, since you cannot be both, and you cannot avoid choosing."

Your personal style is either a carrot, or it is the stick. You prefer to push or pull. When you push, you position is in back of the action, behind those doing the work. The perception becomes, that you are following, not leading the effort. Pushing is counter-productive because it will cause your coworkers to look the wrong direction. Conversely, when you pull, you'll be seen as leading the way. People will find following you easier because, as their pilot, the path becomes very clear. As captain, they will continue to look forward to you, and will shadow your lead.

Unicorn or Rhino - Do You Feel Inspired or Just Motivated?

9

"We all require room for improvement. Thankfully for me, this world is really, really big."

We love to collect things. When we do, it comforts us, making us feel complete. But, we're not complete, and deep down we know this to be true. I'm not perfect and when I make a mistake, I tend to collect these thoughts too. This is a bad pattern and I know it. Remember this; when we make a terrible mistake, that unfortunate act is automatically placed into history by time. It no longer exists. I can't go back and neither can you. We may make amends which can prevent it in the possible future, but it is in the past, and lucky for you and I both, time is waiting.

Unicorn or Rhino - Do You Feel Inspired or Just Motivated?

10

"Excellence is not a measure of any good work. It is a habit that you must practice daily."

I have earned many awards. I'm not boasting, they are just events in my life. I truly love my work, and because I do, I work very hard to make a difference. Each morning that I wake up, I'm hoping to get the chance to inspire others to feel the same way as I do. Even though I know this may be unrealistic, I also realize that if I don't make this attempt, this dream I have will be impossible to achieve. I find it extremely difficult to live calmly with this thought, and so I"ll give it another try. Inspiring others to excellence helps me to see my potential.

Unicorn or Rhino - Do You Feel Inspired or Just Motivated?

11

"Your smile is your logo. Your personality is your product. The feeling you leave others after having spent time with you, is your brand."

I love smiles. I've seen some really great ones, but, I know that your smile is not you. Your smile introduces you to me in a visual way. It may create some fascination for me to desire knowing more about you, but it is not the connection itself. I know that a smile gives only a glimpse of what is inside a person. It is the cover of the book, the shape of a car, or the screensaver on the digital display. Just like your logo, a smile is only a small clue, but still very valuable information. It may be the most important first step you will get to make.

Unicorn or Rhino - Do You Feel Inspired or Just Motivated?

12

"Humans are physiologically, socially, financially, and emotionally motivated beings. We are very complex purchasing machines."

We can easily forget that it is strong, smart, and loyal people that purchase our products, and not vacuous, guilt-ridden robots. Customers will always prefer to think of themselves as strong not weak, smart not ignorant, and loyal not an automaton. They will reject being talked down to, to feel guilty, or pressured. It is dangerous to even try. Should you employ this, they may buy your product or service for some reason, but they will never be faithful to you. Loyalty requires a deep connection built upon trust, and it is always earned.

Unicorn or Rhino - Do You Feel Inspired or Just Motivated?

13

"Inspiration is a spirit, not an action."

Inspiration is not motivation. Inspiration is one of those nebulous concepts that few people understand. Some recall a past memory, or they'll read a historical quote hoping that it will jump-start their day, inspiring them. But, it doesn't, because it can't. Inspiration originates within you, not from without like motivation. The word inspiration, means to "breathe in". You must breathe your passion inside, allowing it to change you, permanently. Anything less than a real inspiration is just a momentary, guilt-produced, societal cup of motivation.

Unicorn or Rhino - Do You Feel Inspired or Just Motivated?

14

"Years from now, we will kick ourselves for focusing so much on STEM to save our future, when what we really needed was some STEAM."

This may come as a shock to hear, but all of the emphasis we place upon STEM classes may become historically inconsequential. Everything that we call STEM may one day be automated systems built by non-human collected data. But, Art adds steam to Science, Technology, Engineering, and Math in a way that has been shown to be super-compelling. Don't misunderstand, I still strongly believe in science and math. While these studies are important to balance the diversity and inclusion in our society, STEAM will always be better.

Unicorn or Rhino - Do You Feel Inspired or Just Motivated?

15

"Hope is not a fantasy as some believe. It is a promise that we keep, to help ourselves to become better."

Hope is not irresponsible, and it is not useless as some might even declare. The reason it is so universally uplifting is that when we hope, we create good memories. These keepsakes that we create, are the very thing that empowers our humanity to tip the scale from deep despair to promise, and from nightmare to daydream. Hope is essential to the future of humanity. It is a solemn promise we make to ourselves. If we weaken it, optimism will die along with our future. Not only should you have hopes, for the sake of mankind, you absolutely must.

Unicorn or Rhino - Do You Feel Inspired or Just Motivated?

16

"Everything looks better from a distance. Your competitor isn't perfect either. Pay less attention to what they are saying and doing, and more to why they are doing it."

We tend to be myopic. This is one of the horrible reasons why we fail. We focus so intently upon the details around us, then we superimpose the same introspective minutiae that we dislike about ourselves, upon our competition. This nearsightedness to which we seem magnetized, keeps us from seeing how our imperfect rivals actually add value, and to what our customers are drawn. Instead, we should be farsighted, focusing upon why they are doing what they are doing, and less upon the particular tactics they are employing.

Unicorn or Rhino - Do You Feel Inspired or Just Motivated?

17

"Imperfection is the result of an object being used outside of its original purpose."

Would you use a pair of scissors as a screwdriver? Hopefully not. You may think this an absurd way to illustrate my point, but strangely, it is a perfect one. We desire so very badly to be a perfect example. It is this fatal attraction we nurture, that will eventually become our kryptonite. We forget that it is not a mistake that the universe made us the way it did. We are all very imperfect for a reason. Superman wasn't perfect either. We been born for a specific purpose, and we can only fail in life, when we struggle to crawl inside of another disguise.

Unicorn or Rhino - Do You Feel Inspired or Just Motivated?

18

"One of life's best solutions for failure, is to put on a fresh shirt and smile."

I know that this isn't some miracle antidote. It may be a superficial formula, and may not the solution we had wished to hear. No, a fresh shirt and a smile can't prevent a future failure. But, it might keep someone interested, long enough for a genuine connection to take place. That reason alone should make smiling important enough for you not to neglect it. A freshly-pressed shirt will make you feel a bit better, and wearing a friendly smile can have a magical way of inviting others to know you even better. So, a smile might help you to succeed.

Unicorn or Rhino - Do You Feel Inspired or Just Motivated?

19

> "Whether you view your customers as one, two, three, or four dimensional, depends upon whether you think about them at your power lunch, or the breakfast table."

Technology surrounds every one of us, even if you happen to live in a very small town. Even if that town is in a third world country. But, for those of us who clock-in and -out, inside of our binary bubble, we begin our day crunching data bits, connecting these dots by lunch time. This may seem sterile, because it is. We must remember that this "data" is people, not the reverse. When taking the long commute home, take a good look in the rear-view mirror. Those are people in the other cars, and they can make your long drive home more pleasant.

Unicorn or Rhino - Do You Feel Inspired or Just Motivated?

20

"Success or failure is not who we are. It is the thing that changes us into whom we become."

As much as we desire others to see us differently, we are not infallible nor impenetrable. We may think of ourselves as detailed and left-brained, but in reality, we have merely learned to sense, adapt, and co-exist with chaos in an unforgiving, non-linear world. In reality we are just like everyone else on the inside. We are malleable and squishy. When we make these modifications to ourselves; to our personality, our skills, our integrity, our self-discipline, and our ambitions, we will over time become either more valuable, or useless.

Unicorn or Rhino - Do You Feel Inspired or Just Motivated?

21

> "Rights and responsibilities are socially glued together. Once you separate them, someone or something will indeed suffer."

I have often said that rights and responsibilities are socially glued together, and once we separate them, someone or something suffers. We desire the right to do things, but not the responsibilities that may go along. When this occurs, some will need to be accountable for the actions to which they have no outcome. Thanks be to the mature, that keeps the car running, the roads clear, and the snacks packed, so that the journey can be enjoyable, even for those rebellious natives that show us how, why, and when to break the rules.

Unicorn or Rhino - Do You Feel Inspired or Just Motivated?

22

"If you are fearful of leaving home, you will never be able to comprehend the vacation experience."

Being afraid is scary, but it is also painful. I know fear is just an emotion, but it can rouse physically as well. It is unfortunate that anxiety can disable so many of us, holding us back. Fear can even prevent us from trying. Once fear settles within a room in your psyche, like a freeloader it will eat all your favorite food in the fridge, and use your bandwidth to play video games all night. Fear will always be the problem life presents to you. It can indeed be scary, but If you desire to succeed at life in a joyful way, then you must find any way to crush it very hard.

Unicorn or Rhino - Do You Feel Inspired or Just Motivated?

23

> "Success in life will be because of your vision, perseverance, and the friendships you've made along the way."

Can you learn to drive a car from a video game? No? How often have you sat in a corporate training class, wondering why you were there? Most of us will trust ourselves to virtually the same screen training scenarios, even though we know some will learn better hands-on, while others alone in a dark room. What's your way? I'm not being facetious, I am serious. This is exactly how close friends are developed. The types of friends that help you to refine your vision, give you the strength when you need it, and help you to see and to achieve your goals.

Unicorn or Rhino - Do You Feel Inspired or Just Motivated?

24

> "A society that does not value its artistic expressions, is a civilization that does not value itself."

I am serious when I state that society owes its life to artists. Where would our human societies be without the architects, the fashionistas, dentists, gardeners, authors, barbers, auto body techs, designers, or animal groomers? While true that societies could survive without the arts, it would quickly become a tedious and miserable existence. The encouragement that we give to our artistic critical thinkers is what has made our society worthy of humanity. They may challenge our thinking, but they also help to make our ugly world a little more enlightening.

Unicorn or Rhino - Do You Feel Inspired or Just Motivated?

25

"Speaking requires only two things; an opinion, and a voice. Listening demands patience, intellect, wisdom, and ears."

Educators and lecturers speak as though we're relegated to become their audience. It's interesting to me, that listening is the first thing a computer device does before it executes, and yet, it is the very last thing a human wants to do before it executes. Listening is the least utilized and practiced skill in business, and in education. Maybe we can learn something from the products we own. We pride ourselves for rejecting the unemotional characteristics of our devices, but as history has shown us, we can and should learn from anything.

Unicorn or Rhino - Do You Feel Inspired or Just Motivated?

26

"I have never failed, because failure isn't falling down, it is staying down."

Failure is a word used by others to make you feel bad. Never give thought to your potential defeat, for it may come regardless. Success can be found most anywhere. Taking action will do for you what nothing else will. If you can't do a big thing, then absolutely do small ones. Just act. Accomplishing small things every day will set you up for success. Contributing in a micro-scale way will even change your outlook on life. It may provide a youthful momentum you previously could not have imagined were impossible, or you were capable.

Unicorn or Rhino - Do You Feel Inspired or Just Motivated?

27

"Having a low opinion of yourself isn't modesty, it is self-destruction."

Do you remember when you were a kid? You had a big imagination, amazing and free. And then you grew up, and disasters piled on. Insecurity feels a lot like this. It isn't, but it can surely feels that way; when you fail a test, when you're rejected by the team, when you miss a goal. These small bites in your psyche nibble away at your confidence. But you actually didn't fail at all. It just wasn't supposed to happen, or the situation timing was horribly wrong. Reminding yourself that you are unique and have real value is a precondition to success.

Unicorn or Rhino - Do You Feel Inspired or Just Motivated?

28

"Be careful what things you carry. It won't be the steep climb that will urge you to give up. It will be the rocks in your shoes."

One of life's biggest lessons is to learn when to let things go. Here's where honesty should become your best friend. This is the painful part where the vision you create in your mind, will clash with your present-day reality. When we hold on to things we shouldn't, we're wearing the same shoes, with the same stones inside. The same shoes worn on the rocky path on your disastrous trek. And so, we end up hating ourselves, our failures, and those around us, instead of learning from this and placing on a new pair every time we take a new journey.

Unicorn or Rhino - Do You Feel Inspired or Just Motivated?

29

"Although we cannot change fate, we can change how we feel about what has happened. This is the singular key that will unlock our future."

Our past is a memory, our future is hidden, and our today is just what it is. I am sure you've heard sayings similar to this before. This isn't just a glib quote. It is truth. We can't change the past, predict the future, and much of the time our "now" is a big blurry mess. There is only one part in this we have any control over — how we feel about either of them. Although there is so much we cannot change about life, we can change how we feel about what has happened to us. In fact, our feelings are the only thing that we can change.

Unicorn or Rhino - Do You Feel Inspired or Just Motivated?

30

"It's not enough to stay in touch with your customers. You must pursue them, consistently telling them how great they are."

If you have a position in sales, marketing, advertising, or customer service, then you should live by this quote. If you don't work in any of these roles, but you're in manufacturing, medical care, construction, or you work for any company, then his phrase should still be exceedingly important. When we work, we design things, build things, do things, service things, and we share things with humans, which makes people your important customers. They should be assured how much you appreciate them, or one day you'll be out of a job.

Unicorn or Rhino - Do You Feel Inspired or Just Motivated?

31

"Save the jokes until you've earned the laughs."

Life can create unwanted stress. This anguish or torment that we sense, trigger our nervous system to open a valve for needed relief. This is why people can burst out into laughter at a funeral and watching a scary movie, or they'll cry at a happy wedding. Emotions require some form of a release for which we may not have full control. Forcing a laugh or a cry prematurely, or preventing them from occurring, can cause another set of undesirable issues. Human emotions are important because they tell a true story. Accept and learn something from them.

Unicorn or Rhino - Do You Feel Inspired or Just Motivated?

32

> "Without fail, making an effort in any situation is pivotal. I'd rather be found wrong, than to be called lazy."

Maybe the word "lazy" is wrong for me to use. Automaker Walter Chrysler was once known to say, "find a lazy man to do a difficult job, since a lazy one will spot an easier way to accomplish the same task." He may just have been on to something. Although a lethargic person may find a quicker way to do an identical task, careful study of their approach may reveal hidden methods that can be modified to boost everyone's performance levels, and their mood. The virtue found here is that there is merit found everywhere, if you know where to look.

Unicorn or Rhino - Do You Feel Inspired or Just Motivated?

Unicorn or Rhino - Do You Feel Inspired or Just Motivated?

33

"Remember that your honest opinion stands directly between ignorance and understanding."

Humans are not binary beings. We may claim to live in the world of on or off, truth or falsehood, but the ubiquitous gray areas are where we set up camp and exist in life. People want to know where you "stand" on a subject, not what the truth is. They want to know what you like and dislike, and why. Here is why A.I. (artificial intelligence) is so difficult to bring into our everyday lives. We seek opinions that make sense to us, not theory or platitudes. We want to be heard, and desire to be persuaded too, but only with our own style of logic.

Unicorn or Rhino - Do You Feel Inspired or Just Motivated?

34

> "Branding is karma. The energy you share, always returns three-fold; financially, experientially, and emotionally."

In Hindi and Buddhism, karma can be defined as a principle of cause and effect, where the intent and actions of an individual, influence their future. This tenant is also found in the biblical new testament, "whatsoever a man sows will he also reap", which you may have heard before. This thought is not new. It is a principle that crosses boundaries and theologies. Branding, marketing, sales, manufacturing, and even finance have actions with deeply embedded repercussions for which we must maintain an acute awareness.

Unicorn or Rhino - Do You Feel Inspired or Just Motivated?

35

"Curiosity may kill the cat, but it will animate dead sales."

"Curiosity killed the cat", is an old Anglo-Saxon proverb, meaning to warn of the dangers of unnecessary investigation or experimentation. It is also basic human nature to be curious. Curiosity is the driving force in our youth that motivates us to explore new ideas, create new experiences, and to discover new ways of doing old things. This is key in the learning process. Sadly, we can lose this youthful inquisitiveness as we grow into adulthood. Equally so, as companies mature, they can neglect the significant importance of curiosity.

Unicorn or Rhino - Do You Feel Inspired or Just Motivated?

36

> "When passion outweighs compassion, you'll end up seeing a forest, instead of trees."

Which is more important, one student or the entire class? What if one student holds back the rest of the class from advancing? Does this make the question any easier for you to answer? Without compassion firmly attached to passion, any zealous act is automation. Like, clearing a large forest of trees with complete disregard for Bristlecone Pines and Harlequin Toads in its path, empathy is key to holistic productivity. We are not groups of walking heads, wandering aimlessly around with nondescript bags over our brain boxes. We're individually united.

Unicorn or Rhino - Do You Feel Inspired or Just Motivated?

37

"Science cannot explain art, but art can decode science."

One of our greatest minds in history, was Albert Einstein. What some may be unaware about him was that he employed mathematical phraseology, or symbols, only after he resolved his problems through imagined images, drawings, or melodic expressions. He rarely thought in words at all. When an artistic concept would come to him, he would first try to express it visually, then at a later time into mathematical computations. This process of creating art is so powerful, it helped him to illuminate the metaphysical natures of the invisible universe.

Unicorn or Rhino - Do You Feel Inspired or Just Motivated?

38

"Branding is not about turning mesmerized heads. Its overriding goal is to raise enlightened eyebrows."

If you're in business, then you should care about branding. And, if you care about branding, then you should care about your customers. If you care about your customers, then you should care what they think. If you care what your customers think, then you'll be fantastic in business. Having a true understanding of what branding actually is, and what it is not, is one of the lynchpins in a successful career. Branding is never about shining a light on your company or product. It is shining that light on your customer.

Unicorn or Rhino - Do You Feel Inspired or Just Motivated?

39

"Creative people never see work as a project or as an assignment. They see it as breathing."

Once you've taken a breath, where has it gone? When you think of it in this way, it seems magical. Breathing gives new life and appears to take nothing in return. There are other things like this in life. For instance, it amazes me that the origins of math are visible everywhere in the cosmos, but, wherever art appears, math seems to disappear. Unless you are Albert Einstein, it may seem impossible for you to observe math and art at the same time, but it is art that breathes life into math, displaying its great mysteries and enchantments.

Unicorn or Rhino - Do You Feel Inspired or Just Motivated?

40

"Imagination does not sell, but it can explain why you are inspired to create things, and why your customers wish to buy them."

Did you need your first bicycle, skateboard, prom dress, or touch-screen cellular phone? Probably not, but you wanted it. When the first microwave oven arrived in stores, most of us were captivated by this new technology enough to purchase one. Creating an interest may be a very important element in marketing, even if you are selling yourself to an employer, or new life partner. But, it is the background story you tell that links "want" and "need" to create imagination. Ensure there is a storyline in every single message.

Unicorn or Rhino - Do You Feel Inspired or Just Motivated?

41

> "A moral compass is vital to success. When we loosen the grip on our values we are likely to lose everything that is commonly linked to them."

Very few companies will identify a moral code as essential to business success. Instead, they will consider corporate prosperity as being built from the tactics, teamwork, and partnerships they've developed. But, corporate ethics are more consequential than the close work relationships they have developed over time. Your values describe you, giving insight into your thinking, what you hold as personally valuable, and the types of customers, or friends you are likely to attract and esteem. Values are the glue that binds all of these people to you.

Unicorn or Rhino - Do You Feel Inspired or Just Motivated?

42

> "We are all the same stardust. We just happened to land in different piles."

You are amazing! I am sure you've heard this said by a friend or family member. If you're lucky you might have even heard this from a coworker or manager. But, in either case, have you considered it might be true? Even though you should, I can understand why you may have trouble believing it. What defines us as unique in the world also marks us as odd. Very few of us have been able to withstand the social pressures of this type of signature, and yet, this specialness that you embody is what should give your life purpose and passion.

Unicorn or Rhino - Do You Feel Inspired or Just Motivated?

43

"The goal should not be to get people to think, but to re-think. More importantly, to imagine."

This book wasn't written to help leaders to become smart or successful. Nor was it was it meant to educate marketing teams to create more memorable advertising campaigns. Although it may result in these, my motive was to help guide spirit-filled leaders, with the tools to better inspire others. Why is this important to me? Because if you remove education, wealth, and success, humanity is all we have left. And, if there is one single thing that humans super-excel in doing, it is imagining a better future. In this, inspiration wins every time.

Unicorn or Rhino - Do You Feel Inspired or Just Motivated?

44

> "Every person has value.
> Every job has importance.
> Every transaction is
> worth the time."

When someone doubts they have worth, there is a resulting constraint in their efforts. They'll stop trying because they only determine their value from the possibility of success. A majority of people do not build their personal values upon the realities of life, but upon their possibilities in life. This bias is bad in a company, and in a relationship. Your goal should always be to understand and appreciate what each person can potentially kindle. The unique variance they hold may be the formula to their eventual success, and also to yours.

Unicorn or Rhino - Do You Feel Inspired or Just Motivated?

45

"Truth exists — and while it can be discovered, it is not created."

Sharing truth is infinitely easier than defining it. What is it that makes truth, true? Snow may be white and grass green, but only if they are at the time. Opinion isn't truth. Theory isn't truth. Ideas are not truth. And, inasmuch as we might want to believe so, realism is not truth either. Truth is not a point of view you put forth, or a belief you may have. It just is. Any message you craft that is meant to flatter or deceive, aims at something other than truth. I don't mean that there is no place for admiration, just make certain that it is true.

Unicorn or Rhino - Do You Feel Inspired or Just Motivated?

46

"If you feel trapped, then change your direction. Remember that there is no such thing as a perpetual motion machine."

When the company I loved, had lost their original dedication, so did we, its workers and customers. I can say that I loved this company and their products. I was sentimentally invested, which made it so terribly crushing for me. Their vision is what made them uniquely desirable. I expected them to savor continued success, and so it was painful for me to watch them fall into the same bad habits. In time, customers would forget why they'd been attracted in the first place. Life changes. Nothing impedes you from changing along with it.

Unicorn or Rhino - Do You Feel Inspired or Just Motivated?

47

"Successful people create lemonade from lemons, and mountains from mole hills. They are exceptional only because they find a way to make something from nothing."

The reason we designate certain people in the world successful, is because the rest of us have collectively decided that these special ones are able to do something that the rest of us cannot. When you think about that in these simplified terms, that leaves the door to success wide open for the rest of us. That might include a caring teacher, a punctual soccer Mom, or your postal carrier who never forgets your name. Most of us can admit to being good at one simple thing. A cool glass of water on a hot day is better than anything else.

Unicorn or Rhino - Do You Feel Inspired or Just Motivated?

48

"Is your glass half empty, or is it half full? A better question might be, are you thankful for your glass?"

Research has shown that the capacity to be thankful is consistently coupled with greater personal happiness. Gratitude allows you to experience positive emotions, relish good experiences, better care for your health, helps you to deal with adversity, and build stronger personal relationships. Positivity (or negativity) is not rooted to our DNA, but must be cultivated, providing social and economic benefits. This positive energy culture we develop, over time can enhance our quality of life, and increase our overall sense of well-being.

Unicorn or Rhino - Do You Feel Inspired or Just Motivated?

49

"Never waste the precious spirit of youth, on the young."

You will grow old soon enough. On the day you first realize this, you will have imperceptibly switched sides. Without you becoming aware of it, age will have begun to raise its resentful head, youth and wisdom will no longer live and work in harmony as they were originally intended. Deceiving themselves to conclude that they must be opponents, both fringes will work separately and independently, misleading themselves to believing that being disjoined, they are smarter, or stronger, or both. Then, all of a sudden, humanity loses.

Unicorn or Rhino - Do You Feel Inspired or Just Motivated?

50

"To every dog, its person is Alexander the Great, Albert Einstein, and Julia Child, all rolled into one. This is why we love them. They see the very, very best in us."

We can learn a great deal from our pets. It is a fact that canines interact with humans differently than any other animal. Dogs cause the human brain to produce a hormone referred to as the "cuddle chemical", increasing our feelings of relaxation and empathy while reducing stress and anxiety. Dogs never judge you for what you wear or the food that you give them. They will stay by your side in a hard rain, or when it is cold. They trust and believe in you, admiring the amazing part of you that no one else in the world recognizes.

Unicorn or Rhino - Do You Feel Inspired or Just Motivated?

51

"Art is one of the fundamental building blocks of civilization. And, while true that society could survive without the arts, life would quickly become a tedious and incredibly miserable existence."

My overriding point here is simple. Never view art as tangental. It is in fact, elemental to civilization. Scientific studies have discovered that inspiration invites regions of the brain to temporarily allow for intercommunication. The barriers between cells are removed, allowing for new collaboration and innovation, and creativity floods into many more regions of the brain's divided nerve areas. This enables neurons to, not only communicate to each other, but to work as a team, on one collaborative single goal. We need far more of this today.

Unicorn or Rhino - Do You Feel Inspired or Just Motivated?

52

"There are so many big things that we can accomplish, in the very small things that we do."

History has recorded many amazing discoveries, in science, math, in the arts, and in language. Every culture has benefited from those having this aptitude to change the world. It is easy to forget that these genius' were youths at one time, just like you and I. They did not raise themselves, feed themselves, guide themselves growing up. Neither did they educate themselves as they began their life journey. They needed loving parents, protective bus drivers, and inspiring teachers, all who knew the value in life's small details.

Unicorn or Rhino - Do You Feel Inspired or Just Motivated?

53

"It is always more difficult to change direction, than it is to stay on an established path."

This is an unshakable truth to which we can testify. Changing direction can be difficult, because it comes with uncertainties. These variables are what scare us the most. Since altering this cycle feels disruptive, human inertia sets in, and the next thing we know we end up in the same place we had begun. These are uncomfortable changes, but they may bring you to a new path, to meet incredible new friends, to a new work environment, potentially to a new residence where you will first meet your brand new unborn potential.

Unicorn or Rhino - Do You Feel Inspired or Just Motivated?

54

"Anger searches for the smallest spot to hide, and once it finds a place to call home, it starts a family."

Have you noticed how focused you become when you are angry? It's bizarre. Our emotional alarm triggers the body's fight or flight response. Your adrenal glands flood the body with stress hormones, and the brain diverts blood away from your organs, to the muscles, in preparation for an immediate physical exertion. This is misplaced readiness. The bulk of us don't live in a place that requires rage to defeat danger. Unfortunately, these hormones stand ready in us, instantly leading to uncontrollable outbreaks, and a damaged self-esteem.

Unicorn or Rhino - Do You Feel Inspired or Just Motivated?

55

"When you come to a fork in the road, the very first thing you should do, is to look for a spoon."

We have problems that arise, requiring decisions that will affect others. Some of these will require out-of-the-box solutions that are not so easily identifiable. Once you reduce your alternatives to age or gender, race or region, PhD or GED, physical beauty or discernible defect, you will constrain your success by the limitation of your potential outcomes. The most innovative and powerful brands clearly understand the influence that diversity imparts to decision-making, and they fiercely protect it as one of their most valuable resources.

Unicorn or Rhino - Do You Feel Inspired or Just Motivated?

56

> "The most powerful forces in nature are chaos and creation. One tears apart, the other brings things together. One is motivation, and the other is inspiration."

Some see evolution as a force. I do not, because it does not require personal contribution in order for change to occur. Evolution merely requires a series of events to happen in a certain sequence. Any resulting change that occurs may not be what you had hoped would materialize. Chaos and creation remain. In chaos mode (or motivation), you are not thinking objectively, you are only reacting to outside forces pressuring you. Only a revolutionary creative mind has the ability to inspire a positive change in others, and enable them to lead.

Unicorn or Rhino - Do You Feel Inspired or Just Motivated?

57

> "Failure is either the cold, hard bedrock you lay prone upon, or it is the stubbornly solid foundation from which your dreams can build."

Most people have experienced how it feels to take a hard fall. It hurts. You can remember the emotions from that circumstance for a long time. Even though the physical pain has past, you can instinctually recall every bruise. Sadly, you will retain it emotionally, also. This reflex is what can hold our backs firmly to that wall. Frightened to move, and yet feeling the safety of the cold slab, we can be our own worst enemy. But, if you consider this block as a foundation, your imagination can inspire you to build a new dream on it.

Unicorn or Rhino - Do You Feel Inspired or Just Motivated?

58

> "Math may have gotten us safely into space and back home again, but it took an artist to dream that it could happen."

Whether you are an accountant, an engineer, or an entrepreneur, it is in your best interest to exploit artists and their strange logic to a greater degree. Invite one of them to your planning session, or even to lunch. They deserve better, and so do you. Their methods may bend your sensibilities, but together the two of you may create a unique way to dialog, and thereby come up with a novel approach to a few of your super-intensely annoying cans of worms. Never think of art as a novel imagination. It is not at all. Art is re-imagination.

Unicorn or Rhino - Do You Feel Inspired or Just Motivated?

59

"I prefer to think of people
as stained-glass windows.
I will only recognize their most
important features when I can
perceive the light that is
coming from behind them."

Spend ten minutes a day with someone different. Talk about this time with others, and encourage each to accomplish goals. It takes so little effort for you to become a center point for their imagination. When people around you feel inspired to succeed, they'll tend to return to you. Some very great ideas come from the least likely places. If, or when, that huge blockbuster idea occurs within your group of acquaintances, you will be there, one of the first to hear it, because you'll be at the epicenter of their imagination.

Unicorn or Rhino - Do You Feel Inspired or Just Motivated?

60

"Many people feel failure as a hammer. I prefer to see it as a feather, a soft reminder that I have not succeeded this time, but I am still here, always ready to try it again."

We hate the idea of failure, even the thought of it. Not merely because of the eventual outcome, but from how defeat reflects directly upon us in our society. But, perspective is important, don't you think? Let me give you an example. Let's say you were unsuccessful thousands of times but on your last try you were am enormous success. People might not even remember your previous disasters. Do you remember any of the failures of Oprah, Stephen King, Walt Disney, J.K. Rowling, or Colonel Sanders? View your failures as light as a feather.

Unicorn or Rhino - Do You Feel Inspired or Just Motivated?

61

"Products and customers are coupled by both a moral consciousness and social awareness. You must have the same qualities if you want to connect with them."

It doesn't matter what you do to make a living, or if you have a brand. It is vital for you to know that. Everything you do and say reflects on you. Your brand is to business what words are to humans. It is the first step in dialog with your customers and coworkers. Both you and your workplace are in the business of social dialog whether you choose to believe it true or not. Every task you conceive, every plan you assemble, and every action you take, says a very great deal to others about what you value as important.

Unicorn or Rhino - Do You Feel Inspired or Just Motivated?

62

"Setting emotional chords is vital to your brand, because the most important and lasting moments in life are never seen, but felt."

Love may be the single most important concept in humanity. Take a moment to think about all of the things that we love to love; like food, music, partners, reading, our cars, our homes, the grandkids, the smell of flowers and fresh cut grass, our pets, and even our work. This list could go on forever. My point is, love is significant to us because we are emotional beings that feel much more than we observe. These emotions are but memorable moments that we string together to employ and connect in a deeper and in much more deliberate way.

Unicorn or Rhino - Do You Feel Inspired or Just Motivated?

63

> "Prior to making a decision, it is beneficial to take a step backward or forward, left or right, up or down."

How do you evaluate an important decision prior to deciding? Few of us take the quality of time required. Notice I didn't say quantity of time, I said quality. This difference is pivotal. Spending too much time (or too little) may not be the distinction between a good or a bad decision. The sufficient amount of quality time, however, is always the right amount, no matter the length. In order to discern the quality, though, will take being open to a new perspective; someone else's, some other place, or at another time.

Unicorn or Rhino - Do You Feel Inspired or Just Motivated?

64

"People may know you, but a dog understands you. Forget becoming a doctor, a rich entrepreneur, or an attorney, when I grow up, I want to be a dog."

Do you remember the original Disney movie, "The Shaggy Dog"? I loved nearly everything about that '59 film. When I stated I want to be a dog, I didn't mean that I wished I actually were a dog. What I meant was that if could become the best part of a dog; it's understanding, gratefulness, and faithfulness, those might be good goals, don't you think? Dogs don't just love you when it is time for dinner. Dogs seem to know when you need a hug, a laugh, or a break from your busy day. How can this thought reenergize your view of work and play?

Unicorn or Rhino - Do You Feel Inspired or Just Motivated?

65

"Fame has two elements, admiration or popularity. Admiration is approval persuaded by a collective respect. Popularity is governed by the private members of an insiders ego contest."

There is absolutely nothing wrong in desiring to be admired, to be wealthy, to possess skills, or even worldly fame. But ultimately, what most of us truly wish, is to achieve our own distinct aspiration in life, to feel secure in the knowledge of our unique purpose, realizing how we fit into the big picture. Avoid popularity if you can, for it will only draw you inwards, pushing that monstrous social angst inside of you to even deeper depths, all the while hiding it with a shiny grin, to where people will become less significant.

Unicorn or Rhino - Do You Feel Inspired or Just Motivated?

66

"Never judge ability,
by disability."

Humans are inclined to reject mechanization as mostly being heartless and cold. Technology is prominent in our culture, and yet, we will hold an even lesser value for those with defective motor neurons. Evidently, this manner in which some of us move about, can strike many of us as imperfect. How we move from place to place, whether by horse cart, Maserati, or by wheelchair, can be the difference if your ideas are considered, accepted, or even noticed. Apparently, it is evident that our robots may just be lightyears ahead of us.

Unicorn or Rhino - Do You Feel Inspired or Just Motivated?

67

"The reason that Hope is so universally uplifting, is that these visions we nurture are the things that keep our humanity tipping the scale from despair to promise, from nightmare to daydream."

Without the initial dream, there would be no hope. And without hope, no vision. Hope gives power to dreams, and dreams provide the roadmap for your vision. A vision may indeed be the vehicle that enables dreams and hopes to move, but without dreams and hopes, a vision would be a motionless transport without the fuel to explore, or the comfort to enjoy the trip. All things may indeed be hinged to a dream, but hope is the ultimate adhesive that binds the dreams and visions of humanity firmly together while moving.

Unicorn or Rhino - Do You Feel Inspired or Just Motivated?

68

"As a former high school teacher, I knew that I might be able to motivate twenty students at a time, but I could only inspire one at a time."

Things can go horribly wrong for us when we feel guilty for not becoming what we have observed somewhere else. We're not a mental genius, strong, we're too short or tall. We're impaired, or a color we don't like, or we've been denied that promotion we've worked so long and so hard to attain. These motivations are counter productive. If you feel pressured to meet another's goals, you are only motivated. Inspiration, on the other hand, lives inside of you, where you're so focused upon joy, you're a revelation to others.

Unicorn or Rhino - Do You Feel Inspired or Just Motivated?

69

"There are times when people need someone else to help them see the part of themselves that a mirror cannot show."

When we look at ourselves in a mirror, we see something different from what others see, other than our less than obvious physical faults, which we are keenly aware. We'll view ourselves skewed from reality. We'll see someone with few or countless talents, a torrid past or boundless future, someone with lessor or greater options. Some will see the truth while others will have a super positive, almost prideful position about our looks, skills, and options. This notions confirms the prime importance of keeping true friends close.

Unicorn or Rhino - Do You Feel Inspired or Just Motivated?

70

"Mom was right. Gratitude does not end, but it begins, with attitude."

Are you happy? A more appropriate question might be, are you grateful, because happiness is relative. Without making any verdict or conclusion about your personal situation, I can assure you that, in general, people will never tell the truth about their state of happiness. In addition, there are so many variables to happiness, making its measure exceedingly difficult. One emotion we can quantify though, is gratefulness. It is measurable. We know when a person is truly grateful because of the amount given back in return.

Unicorn or Rhino - Do You Feel Inspired or Just Motivated?

71

"Listening is one of the least utilized and valued indicators in education. Believe it or not, branding is education."

Over the centuries, the world has conditioned us to value speakers to a greater degree than listeners. We honor noted lecturers, are attentive to our professors, we stay awake for priests and pastors, gaze at musicians, and repose contented for the sublime words of our politicians. In doing so, we have been reduced to becoming an applaudience. Branding should never employ this unholy strategy, for the most powerful brand messages that you craft, should inspire your customers to speak out loud and clear.

Unicorn or Rhino - Do You Feel Inspired or Just Motivated?

72

"As much as we desire others to see us differently, we're not born hard and impenetrable. In truth, we're malleable and squishy."

Do you remember playing with modeling clay? It was brownish-gray in color. I'm sure you might have when you were a child in school. The dinosaur you made could be treasured or it could be refashioned into a sports car within minutes. At the end of the day it could be stored in a plastic bag, ready for tomorrow's fascination. It can be overlooked that we are a lot like this clay. Our personality, skills, and passions can be refashioned. Not as simple as me saying it, but it is possible. Your life is just like that little ball of brown clay.

Unicorn or Rhino - Do You Feel Inspired or Just Motivated?

73

"If you want to build a long lasting, successful brand, begin with honesty."

You may see yourself as a leader one day, so here is a very important tip: Great leaders never cheat to get to the top. Leaders do, but not the great ones. You can be successful and not be great. Honesty is coupled by integrity. Integrity means you attempt to do the right thing because it is the right thing, not the only thing. An honest brand tells the truth and expects it in return, from its employees and customers too. An honest brand never fattens the truth, or winks. Its ethical values are at stake. You mean far to much to them.

Unicorn or Rhino - Do You Feel Inspired or Just Motivated?

74

"Branding is not image building. It is tethering a set of emotions, so that your customers can both understand and identify with your products and goals."

Branding not what you many think. Advertising creates attention. Promotion creates drive. Marketing is image, sales, and distribution. Diversely, branding will generate what advertising, promotion and marketing cannot. Branding doesn't reinforce a product or service. Branding creates a soul. A strong brand will permeate human emotions, developing a human-like character, and embedding loyalty deep within your product. More than monetary monarchs, real brands will be chosen and honored as societies pioneers.

Unicorn or Rhino - Do You Feel Inspired or Just Motivated?

75

"Power brands know that an empty stomach will never listen to what you have to say."

People may vote with their wallet, but they will rise in revolt with what they sense in their stomach. This is a political truth. If you wish to predict where political instability, revolution, or a corporate coup d'etat will occur, the best determinant is how often your countrymen are fed. As long as there's food in their stomach, they will listen. This is also a lesson for those who brand. You cannot feed the hungry on statistics. It isn't enough for customers to hear how great you are, they must hear how amazing you think they are.

Unicorn or Rhino - Do You Feel Inspired or Just Motivated?

76

"You may not be a social disrupter or a game changer, but you're probably not a complete failure either."

Setting goals for yourself is essential to your vision, and missing just one goal can feel crushing. Failing is not the end of the world, although it may certainly feel like it. If so, the world would have ended long ago. Failure does not mean falling down, it is most definitely staying down. As difficult as it can be, get back up. Failure reminds me that I am not perfect, and although I have not succeeded this time, I am still here, bruised but unbroken. In time I'll be ready to give it another go, but this time I'll approach it with a little more joy.

Unicorn or Rhino - Do You Feel Inspired or Just Motivated?

77

"Products are not objects. They have personalities, and just like people, they can be made or be broken in the marketplace."

I love advertising! If done correctly, it is a social dialog. It tells a story. Never forget that there are no 'masses', only people — individuals. Some of the most powerful campaigns may have broken from traditional marketing formulas, and yet, they were successful because they reached out and touched a group of souls, at a very crucial time. Products, just like people, have emotional weight, inherent personalities. to which customers identify and make a part of their family. And just like your household pet, these personal objects are family too.

Unicorn or Rhino - Do You Feel Inspired or Just Motivated?

78

"Your brand is not a product. It is the sum total of what customers know about you."

Your product is not a brand, and your brand is not a product. If you treat them as such, your company will only be a commodity, an object with value. In this scenario, you may indeed sell product, but as a bargain leader it will be hard for you to claim a jubilant victory. Brands have personalities not prices. They have loyalties not obligations, and friends not foes. Customers are faithful to brands not products. Your brand should plainly spell out how, and why you are loyal to your customers. You'll want to become a brand, no matter the cost.

Unicorn or Rhino - Do You Feel Inspired or Just Motivated?

79

> "Branding is just teaching. Education is just informed enlightenment. Your very best brand pitch should simply illuminate choices."

I guess, by now, you can tell how I feel about branding. It's not because I enjoy selling things (I don't), but because storytelling is such a large part of this process. Teaching is exactly the same to me. It is storytelling. The very best teachers I recall from my childhood told us stories to get us to remember important points. And I did. I think this may be why I loved teaching as well as advertising and branding. Stories are why we tune in to music and movies, it is why we love to listen to each other, and it's why the best products sell.

Unicorn or Rhino - Do You Feel Inspired or Just Motivated?

80

> "To revolutionize your business, you must first master the language of your customers. Not what they're saying, but what they mean when they are saying it."

Years ago my neighbor had lost his dog. He was so deeply concerned that his family pet was lost. Trying to help, I asked him the breed because it looked like a spaniel. "No, no,", he said, "it is canine-American". "You're kidding," I said, "it's what?" He seemed so visibly upset by this question, that I genuinely thought he had to be joking, but he wasn't. I didn't understand then, but, I get it now. What others value, we may not recognize. If we desire to know them, we will have to take all of the time that is required to comprehend what it is that they value.

Unicorn or Rhino - Do You Feel Inspired or Just Motivated?

81

"The art of brainstorming, where you're free to embrace whatever sudden thought of neural electrification that inspires you, has evaporated, just like the amazing aroma of freshly baked bread."

A ten-year old once told me that he had regretted entering middle school. He was unapologetic, and very serious. For him, school just wasn't any fun at all. We know now, that excitement is an extremely essential element in this task of learning and problem-solving. If true, then we need this in business. But joy is not on our teams to-do list. Tableau charts have removed all the fun from fundamental, and replaced it with "traction", "competency", and "journey", useless terms that can never top the smell of a steaming hot dog at a ball game.

Unicorn or Rhino - Do You Feel Inspired or Just Motivated?

82

"If you are hell-bent upon becoming a revolutionary leader, you won't see any satisfaction in driving cattle."

A tyrant and a revolutionary are both leaders. Each have dedicated enthusiasts; those who believe in them, and want to follow. A tyrant has ambitions that are destined to meet personal goals. For a tyrant, there will be times, when you, or others, will only be in their way, making you mere game fodder. On the other hand, a revolution has aspirational goals; objectives that are positively powered by inspiration. These tireless and selfless leaders trust their team and their instincts, linking these to your passions, inspiring others to follow.

Unicorn or Rhino - Do You Feel Inspired or Just Motivated?

83

"A good leader will bring a horse to water. A great leader will be one that gives the horse something salty first."

People use this word "salty" to describe a person's emotional condition. When someone appears irritated or are angry they might be described as having a salty disposition. It might also be someone with very memorable experiences, such as a salty sailor might have undergone. Salt is used on ailments too. It has the effect of drawing something out of a person or a thing that had previously been unnoticed. Although it might initially be an unpleasant experience, salt just might help you to enjoy that first big gulp.

Unicorn or Rhino - Do You Feel Inspired or Just Motivated?

84

"If you and your products are not a brand, then you are just a commodity."

You might not want to hear me say this again, especially if you believe that there is absolutely nothing wrong with being a commodity. After all, people like to purchase and keep things readily on hand, So then, what is wrong with being a commodity? I'll tell you. It's not enough just to sell product. Not if you desire to be a brand leader. In your scenario, you may indeed sell product. You may even make a healthy profit. But a bargain leader is not the same as a brand leader, is it? You may survive, but you will not thrive.

Unicorn or Rhino - Do You Feel Inspired or Just Motivated?

85

"You must make the decision to forgive before you can fully understand what forgiveness means. You'll have to stick your hand into the dirt, to plant the seed."

Forgiving someone is difficult, but forgiving yourself is the hardest of all. The fatiguing part is, you must make a firm commitment to forgiveness for it to mean anything, and humans find commitment very difficult. Someone hurts us and we don't want these feelings to be repeated, so we hold grudges and we build walls. It's understandable, but it is also tremendously harmful. In these monumentally stressful moments we should rely on a simple committed decision. Only when we learn commitment, can we move forward and grow.

Unicorn or Rhino - Do You Feel Inspired or Just Motivated?

86

"A society that does not value its artistic expressions, is a civilization that simply does not value itself."

Tell me, who is more entrepreneurial than an artist...more of an artist than an entrepreneur? Both have new ideas, and meet with resistance to change. Both are driven by inspiration and self-motivated to individual success. History has shown us that better than half the time, neither the artist nor the entrepreneur can discern if their future plans will succeed. We love entrepreneurs, but we less than passionately put up with artists. We owe them both a huge gratitude. They are the builders of civilization.

Unicorn or Rhino - Do You Feel Inspired or Just Motivated?

87

> "Rather than sterile, and statistical plots on graph paper, I prefer people to be seen and understood as endlessly moving points of inspirational light."

For those of us who are passionate about branding, this is an important lesson to learn. Our goal should always be to reassure our brand devotees of their choices, and not just quantifying subscribers. These verified packets of customer data that we collect, profiled thought chunks, should not just become a secret database cauldron for our company and their marcom analytical staff. It should be shared with our customers too. They should know why we love their loyalty to us.

Unicorn or Rhino - Do You Feel Inspired or Just Motivated?

88

"Although I consistently attempt to work outside of the box, I always keep one foot in, for good measure."

I'm sure you've heard the saying, "think outside of the box". I also know that doing so is entirely possible, because there are people who've done it. Despite being contrary to belief, successful and revolutionary thinkers do the impossible every day — they find a way to be in two places at once. This is, in fact, essential to innovation, and you can do it too! The key here is to place one foot in a different "thought" box, while retaining your own perspective. If you do, you'll glean important data critical to success.

Unicorn or Rhino - Do You Feel Inspired or Just Motivated?

89

"The next time you feel unworthy or inadequate, remember that these feelings have nothing to do with you. There are no lower or higher individuals in the view of the universe."

The definition of inadequacy is when something is found to be lacking in a desired area, or no longer having a required purpose. This horrible sensation overwrites every other positive decision you make, leaving you to feel hopeless. Most of us have felt this way before, but let me share something significant. There is one thing we can count on, it is that feelings change. We are walking liquid pools of emotion, in constant revision. You can change too. You can also help others to change. We're all needed in order to help each other achieve.

Unicorn or Rhino - Do You Feel Inspired or Just Motivated?

90

"The bottom line should be that customers trust you. If they do not, then you'll at least want them to believe that you trust them."

You own a company, or work for one. You have a family, or are a member in one. Trust is just as important between family members, a it is for your customers. Confidence can be broken. When this occurs, a return to reliance can be nearly impossible to gain back. If friends find it to be insurmountable to trust you in the same way, one possible path back is to show how much you believe and trust in them. I realize that your pride may find this displeasing, but your customers and patrons may need this help to find their way back to you.

Unicorn or Rhino - Do You Feel Inspired or Just Motivated?

91

"It takes more than a great idea. You have to be a leader. They'll call you a leader because you'll also know when it is right to follow."

As ridiculous as this may sound, it is my belief, that leaders will innately fall into one of two categories: they'll keep the pace, or they'll create it. Those who keep it are clock watchers, file savers, and bean counters. They'll keep you honest. They make excellent rule keepers, no, rule guardians! But, those that create it are pack leaders who are able to energize the uninspired, and turn monochrome into technicolor. They look at details as though they're an annoying fly. A leader not only leads, he or she will also know when to follow.

Unicorn or Rhino - Do You Feel Inspired or Just Motivated?

92

"Brand chaos will kill a brand revolution. A brand evolution will kill itself."

You'd probably be able to tell me if your company was in chaos, but could you tell me if your business was evolving, or in a revolution? Remember this: If you are evolving you're not in charge, the process is, and you won't have any control over any change that happens. This process of evolution will have a tendency to convolute your business strategies indiscernibly, while you are in the drivers seat, and sleeping at the wheel. If you want to drive a zealous company of people on a fun trip, you'll need to lead a revolution.

Unicorn or Rhino - Do You Feel Inspired or Just Motivated?

93

"Math is a repudiation of anarchy, while Art is a rebellion against predictability."

Math might have taken us into the universe, but it took an artist to imagine that this could even be possible. Every culture in every land, and in every time, has embraced the creative mind to explain the complexities of the universe, used it to comfort others, and make extremely complicated things simpler to imagine or understand. Art breathes life into a community, and to business. Once artists are allowed to return into a dying urban landscape, fresh oxygen is created, a revitalized business returns, allowing math and science wizards to flourish again.

Unicorn or Rhino - Do You Feel Inspired or Just Motivated?

94

"Branding isn't who you are, what you do, or the size of your media footprint. It is what your customers think about it."

Many of the world's most popular, strong, and enduring brands are built from the heart. This is the cornerstone of power branding, and how you should brand yourself. What are your principles that are worthy of sharing with others? How strongly do you believe in them and why? How do these values you treasure, measure up with mine? Vital questions. Once people believe that you and your company share their standards, they will become and continue to be loyal to you despite what others say. Your brand to be one of those to which they are loyal.

Unicorn or Rhino - Do You Feel Inspired or Just Motivated?

95

"Once or maybe twice in a lifetime, the universe will wink and nod at you at the same time to let you know that you are on the right track. When that happens, wink back."

Serendipity is a marvelous word. I like to think of it as good luck with chocolate sauce and sprinkles on top. I've not had this happen to me many times, and for a good reason too. This type of good fortune should be savored, not expected, like that first bicycle you received. You know, the one with the rainbow streamers coming out of the handlebars. You looked at it, then you looked at everyone else who was looking at you. Incredible. It is times like these when serendipity deserves both a wink, and a nod.

Unicorn or Rhino - Do You Feel Inspired or Just Motivated?

96

"Whenever we make any alterations to ourselves; in our personality, our skills, our self-discipline, and in our ambitions, they will either become priceless, or useless."

We are much more like styrofoam cups than we'd like to think. We're fragile. We hold a variety of hot and cold things and are refreshed by redesigning our outside, as it suits us. When we make these mods to our foam cup — our personality, our skills, our integrity, our self-discipline, and our ambitions may change from being priceless, to become pointless. Whichever decisions you make, remember that any alterations will leave a semi-permanent, underlying mark to your brand that will affect every future imprint upon which you decide.

Unicorn or Rhino - Do You Feel Inspired or Just Motivated?

97

"People trust math and can be confused by art, because math is logical and obvious, while art appears magical and mysterious."

Why have the arts never been given credibility equal to science and math? I will agree that art might be described as instinctual and a bit pretentious, but, here is an interesting observation. Math, by its nature, exists without any regard to humanity, while Art, by its nature, disrupts stability in order to serve humanity. They are so dissimilar, yet, they cohabit the very same place in the universe, equally dependent upon each other. What is even more difficult to discern is that art is very exhaustively written, invisible math.

Unicorn or Rhino - Do You Feel Inspired or Just Motivated?

98

"Guilt, is a house without walls, a floor, chair, or a bed, with absolutely no place to rest."

For many, guilt can be a terribly crushing weight that hovers heavily upon every moment of your day. Unless you are extremely anti-social or psychopathic, you have experienced this. But, this perception can also be an important step in you reclaiming your personal psyche. Guilt may resist change, but it is your choice. Remorse or regret, awakening or re-centering, either will have the sought out effect of stimulating you to make necessary changes in your life. One change loiters inside you. The other moves outward to help others.

Unicorn or Rhino - Do You Feel Inspired or Just Motivated?

99

"Can you speak Latin or Sanskrit? Neither can your customers. Use a language they will understand, enabling them feel smarter, and better to engage with you."

If you desire to lead, then you had better learn to communicate well. When I say "communicate", I mean to engage your customers and staff in a way they can understand. Your goal is not merely to create excitement. It is to share how special your customers truly are. While many TV ads appear to derive from the same boring factory, and auto designs look like the same lifeless econobox, we get bored. No individuality. No personality. It is no wonder that people are so confused. The stories — they are all the same.

Unicorn or Rhino - Do You Feel Inspired or Just Motivated?

100

"We spend far to much time and energy training employees to have answers and to follow, instead of teaching them to inspire others, and to lead."

Although you and I may forever disagree on a number of things, we should be able to agree on this; time has a way of changing grade "A" opportunities, into passing grades, sometimes without us even realizing this change had happened. While companies pat themselves on the back for training incredible recruits to be unemotionally task-focused, they may also be readying them to become the very best employees that a military mill will ever hire. If you desire only the best, you'll need to guide them to be passionate about inspiring others to change lives.

Unicorn or Rhino - Do You Feel Inspired or Just Motivated?

Unicorn or Rhino - Do You Feel Inspired or Just Motivated?

Thank you:

for wanting to enrich your own life,
and potentially the lives of others.
If you have learned anything from
reading this book, please share it.

RandyZ

Unicorn or Rhino - Do You Feel Inspired or Just Motivated?

www.ingramcontent.com/pod-product-compliance
Lightning Source LLC
Chambersburg PA
CBHW060831220526
45466CB00003B/1054